The Business Model Implementation Toolkit

WHAT TOP ENTREPRENEURS USE
TO BUILD AND GROW THEIR COMPANIES

by Josh Ray

The Business Model Implementation Toolkit helps entrepreneurs create a complete business model.

It collects the data on:

- **Who**
    - Customers
- **What**
    - Value Proposition Needs/Wants
    - Channels
    - Customer Relationship Preferences
- **Why**
    - Revenue Streams
- **How**
    - Key Resources
    - Key Activities
    - Key Partnerships
    - Cost Structures

Additionally, adding insights on:

- Knowing **WHO** your customers segments are.

- **WHAT** they want, desire, and need, where they have pains in the business operations, and what gains your business can offer.

- **WHY** they should use your product & services. **WHY** you are better and **WHY** they should choose you.

- **HOW** you can deliver, **HOW** you can serve them, **HOW** your business is better

The 9 Building blocks:

- Customer Segments
- Channels
- Customer Relationships
- Value Propositions
- Revenue Streams
- Key Activities
- Key Resources
- Key Partnerships
- Cost Structure

Determining all of these really creates the vision for your model. You will know what needs to be executed.

When beginning your model, the first and most important building blocks are:

1. Customer Segments
2. Value Propositions

Further insights and understanding can be found in my E-Book **The Entrepreneurs Business Model Implementation Guide**
https://www.amazon.com/Entrepreneurs-Business-Implementation-Laying-Foundation/dp/1707587078/ref=tmm_pap_swatch_0?_encoding=UTF8&qid=1581814535&sr=1-18

Who is your dream customer?

By creating a customer persona, it allows you to fully visualize your dream customer.

A customer persona makes your customer more than a number or a sale. It brings them to life, gives them character and allows for you to know who they are before you ever meet them and serve them. Knowing more about your customer gives great advantages in the success, growth, and longevity of your business.

Giving that, the customers determine the value and the overall profit and revenue of your business. Knowing as much about them as possible will create an experience that makes them feel welcomed and appreciated. By creating a customer persona template, it will create the needed understanding of your dream customers and will allow for you to be ahead of the way their needs will evolve. Being able to adapt to their needs will keep you in front on the competition.

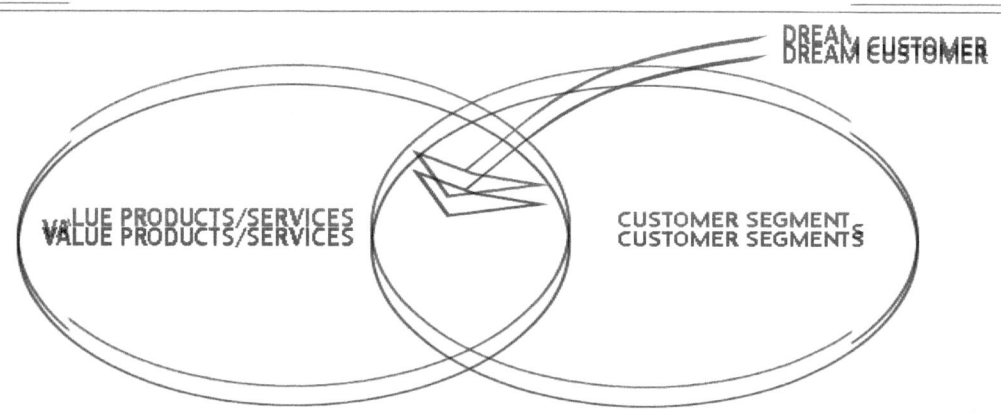

When creating the persona, being as detailed and precise as possible is key. Your customers are more than just a customer. They have lives, jobs, families, interests, hobbies, passions, beliefs, and values. Be sure to add all of these details into your persona template.

Not only is a customer persona important for you to be able to connect to your customer, it is also important for you to know whom you do not want to have as a customer. Though, anyone has the right to be a customer and truly you will do business with anyone. Knowing your dream customer will allow for you to have a strong connection to them. Being able to do this will reduce time wasted on non-serious customers and let you focus on those who are loyal.

Once you have created your customer persona, utilize it in developing your customer journey map.

Each individual customer persona will need an individual customer journey map. These maps can vary in detail. The template provided is a map that covers any and all customer journeys. Knowing whom your customer is and what they experience to lead them to your product or service will help build a trusting customer relationship.

The Tool Kit Purpose:

This Complete Business Model Design Toolkit is designed to create and build your business model starting with your customer and ending with your products/service value ladder for you customers to be funneled through.

This tool kit is useful for any business online or brick and mortar.

What's Included

- Customer Persona Checklist
- Customer Persona Template
- Customer Journey Template
- Empathy Map Template
- Design Thinking Process Outline
- Value Proposition Canvas Template
- Complete Business Model Design Template
- Standard Business Model Canvas
- SWOT Analysis Template
- Value Ladder Template
- Sales Funnel Template
- Cash Flow Quadrant (Bonus)

PERSONA PROFILE CHECKLIST

Persona Detail	Questions to Ask
Role	What is your job role/role in life? Your title? How is your job/role measured? What is a typical day? What skills are required? What knowledge and tools do you use? Who do you report to? Who reports to you?
Company/Organization	What industry or industries does your company work/is your role in? What is the size of your company/organization (revenue; employees)?
Goals	What are you responsible for? What does it mean to be successful in your role?
Challenges	What are your biggest challenges?
Watering Holes	How do you learn about new information for your job? What publications or blogs do you read? What associations and social networks do you belong?
Personal Background	Age; Family (married; children); Education
Shopping Preferences	How do you prefer to interact with vendors? (email; phone; in person) Do you use the internet to research vendors or products? If yes; how do you search for information?

BUYER PERSONA WORKSHEET TEMPLATE

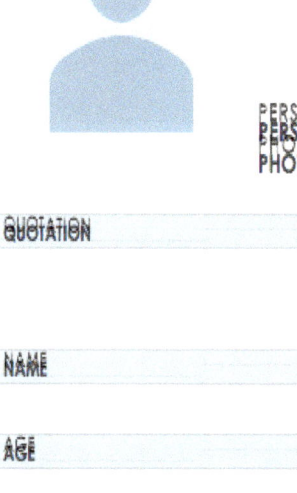

PERSONA PHOTO

QUOTATION	
NAME	
AGE	
GENDER	
LOCATION	
OCCUPATION	
JOB TITLE	
HIGHEST LEVEL OF EDUCATION	
ANNUAL INCOME	

GOALS AND MOTIVATIONS

SALES OBJECTIONS

CHALLENGES AND OBSTACLES

SOURCES OF INFORMATION

- BOOKS
- BLOGS
- CONFERENCES
- EXPERTS
- MAGAZINES
- WEBSITES

What is a Customer Journey Map?

A visualization of a customers' objectives, needs, feelings and barriers throughout the path-to-purchase for a product, service or brand.

	Attract	Interact	Engage	Convert
Objectives	**Trigger a need**	**Understand the need**	**Provide solutions**	**Act**
Needs	• Remind or trigger a need • Recognize I have a problem • Address a pain point	• I don't know what I don't know • Draw me a scenario • I have questions	• Deal with the immediate need • Be relevant • Personalize • Partnership • Privacy/trust	• Clarify • Validate • Satisfaction • Reality
Feelings	• Anxious • Defensive • Distracted • Hopeful	• Ambivalent • Curious • Guarded • Open	• Interested • Frustrated • Excited • Feel good	• Resolved • Loyal • Confident
Barriers	Relevance, trust, fear, acknowledgement, time, convenience, distraction	Style, approach, language, expectations, time, knowledge of client	Literacy, risk tolerance, convenience, time, commitment	

- An Empathy Map is a great way to begin the development of your Design Thinking strategy session.

- Design Thinking is a design methodology that provides a solution-based approach to solving problems.

- It begins with Empathizing with the Problem and ends with Testing the Solution designed.

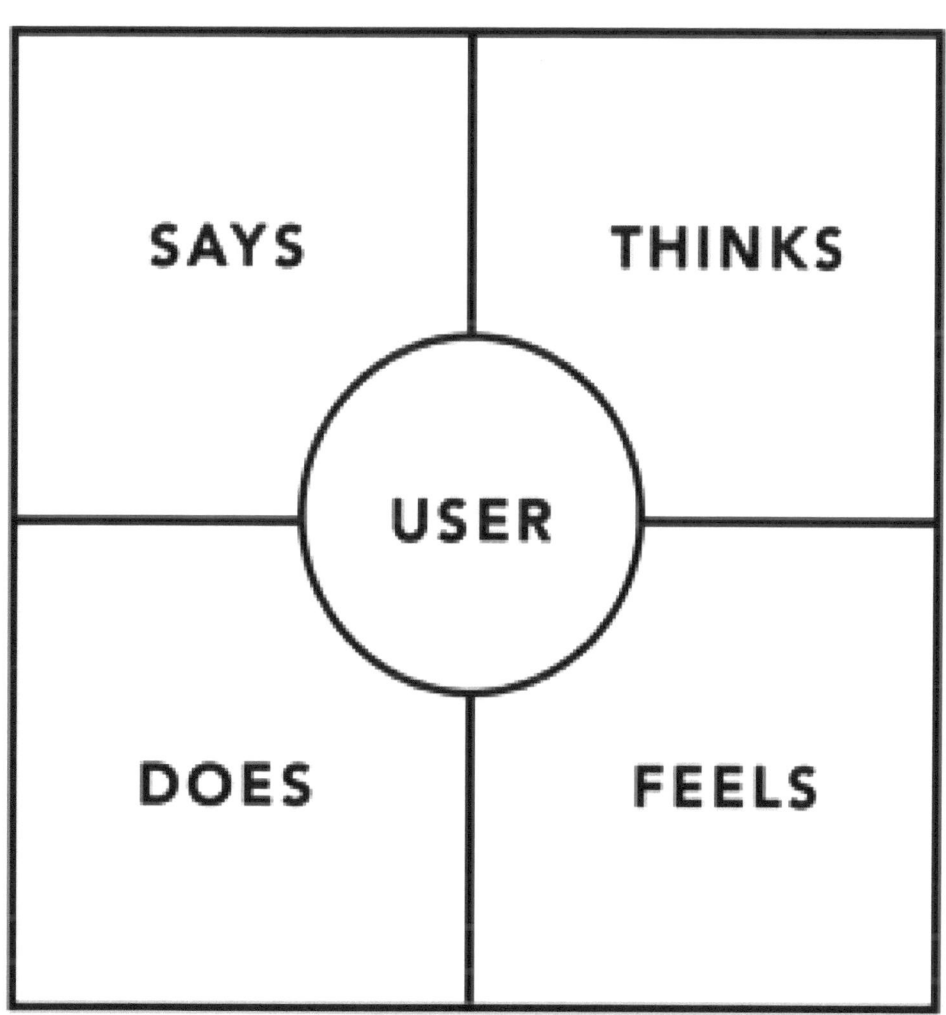

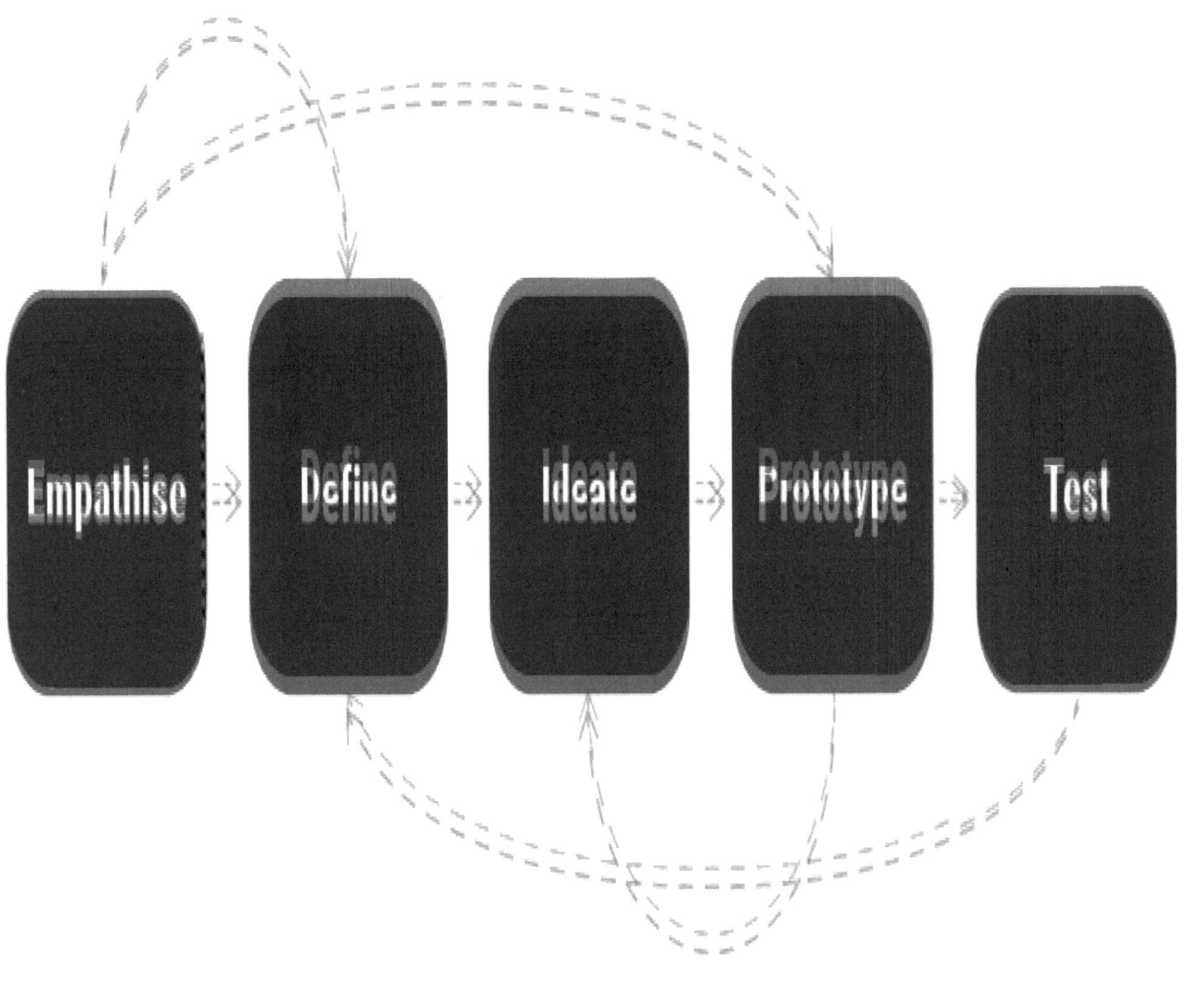

What is a Value Proposition?

Target	Benefit	Differentiation
Who	What	Why

- What is the Market size?
- How do we Identify Potential Customers?

- What features are essential and needed to create success?
- What can be excluded?

- What makes this different than our competitors offers & solutions?
- What is an appropriate Price?

Your Value Proposition Address two things

1. Pain Points
2. Gain Creators

Your Value Propositions can be two things

1. Innovative and represent a new or disruptive Offer
2. Similar to existing market offers, but with added features and attributes, convenience

Values may be

1. Quantitative (e.g. Price, Speed of service)
2. Qualitative (e.g. Design, Customer Experience)

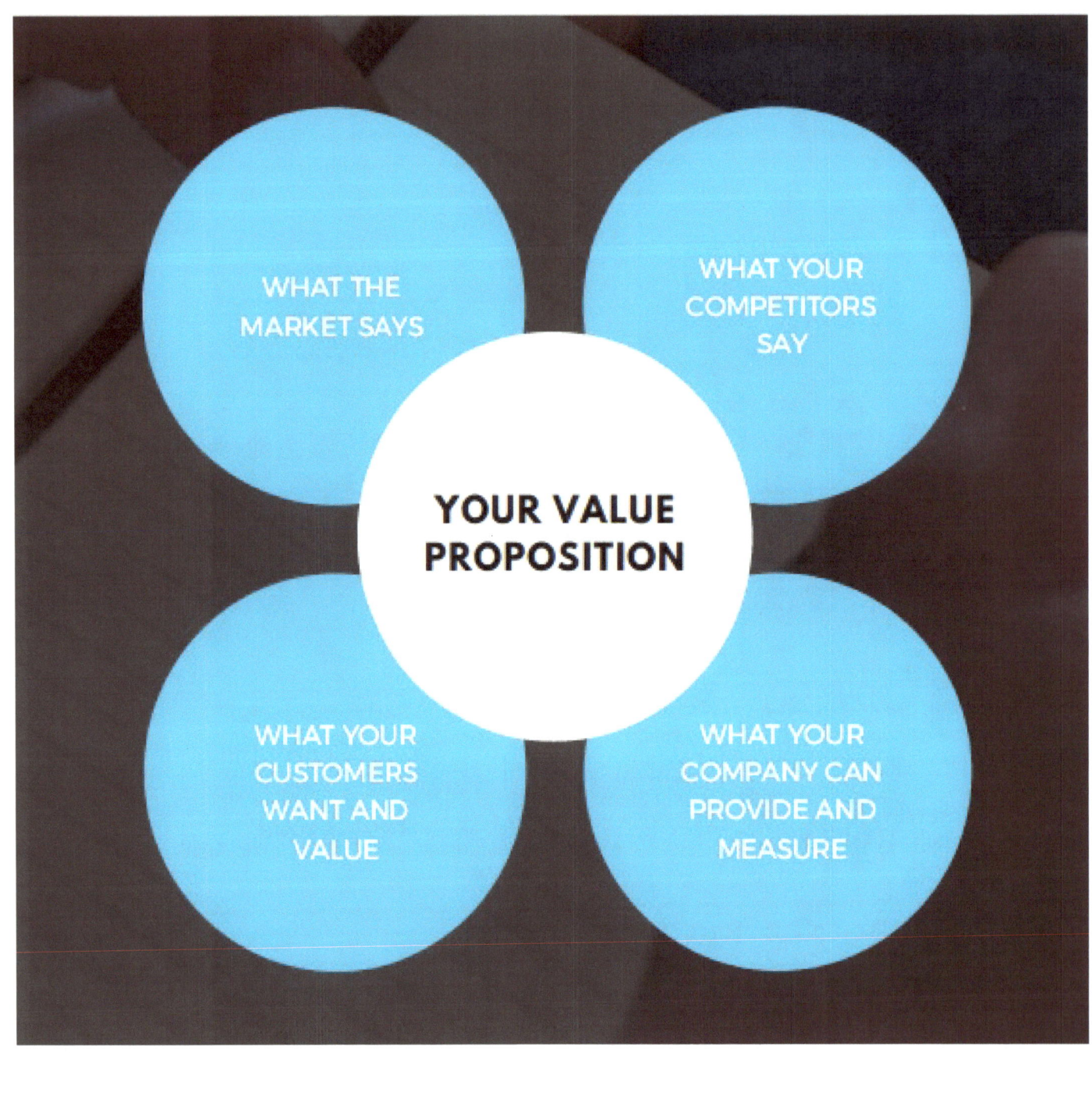

Value Proposition Canvas

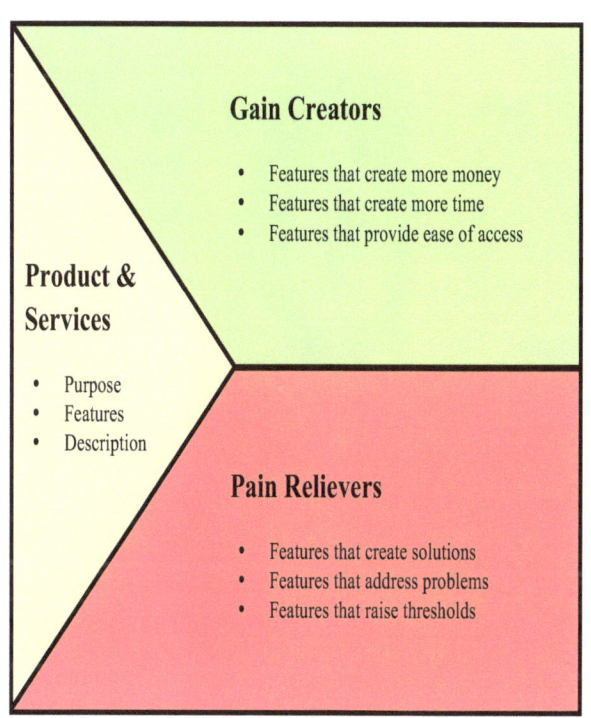
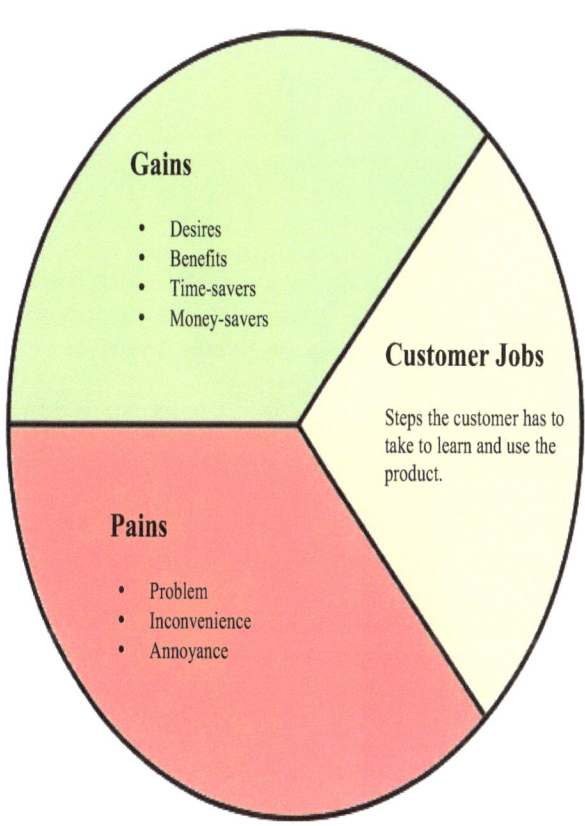

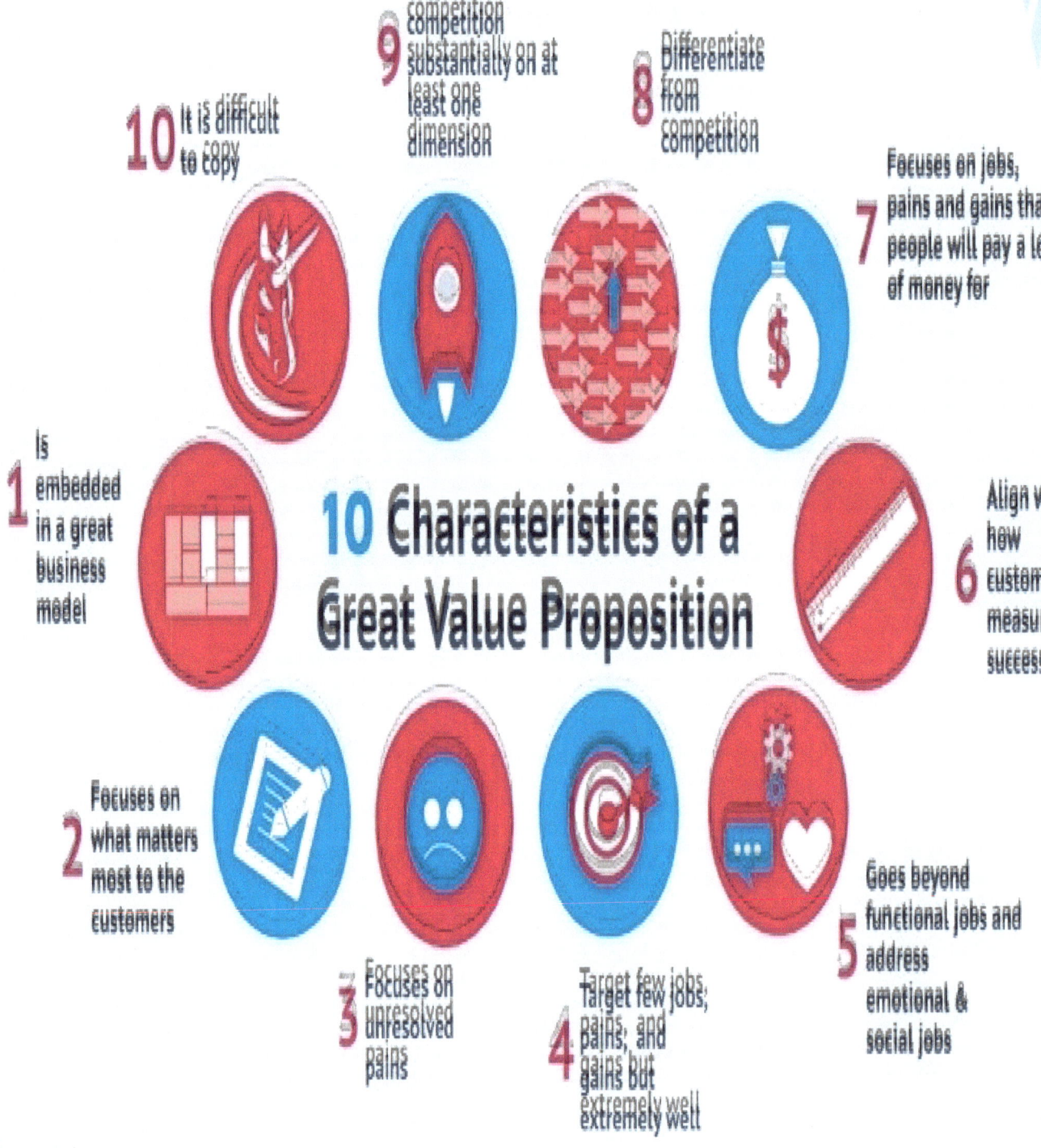

A Value Proposition has 4 essential elements

It shows how products/services create value for a specific <u>customer segment</u>

The customer's perspective	What's in it for them?	Why choose to buy from you?	Prove it
Customer needs and insights	**Promise of value that resonates**	**Competitive Differentiation**	**Proof and quantification**
• What problems do they need to solve? • How can they increase sales? • How can they reduce costs?	• Benefits that add value to your customer • Solving their urgent problems • Why they should care about your solution	• Demonstrate points of difference from your competition that matter to your customers. • Put action plans in place to improve points of parity	• Create trust = why should your customer believe you? • Quantify the benefits in your customers' language

The 20 Minute Business Plan

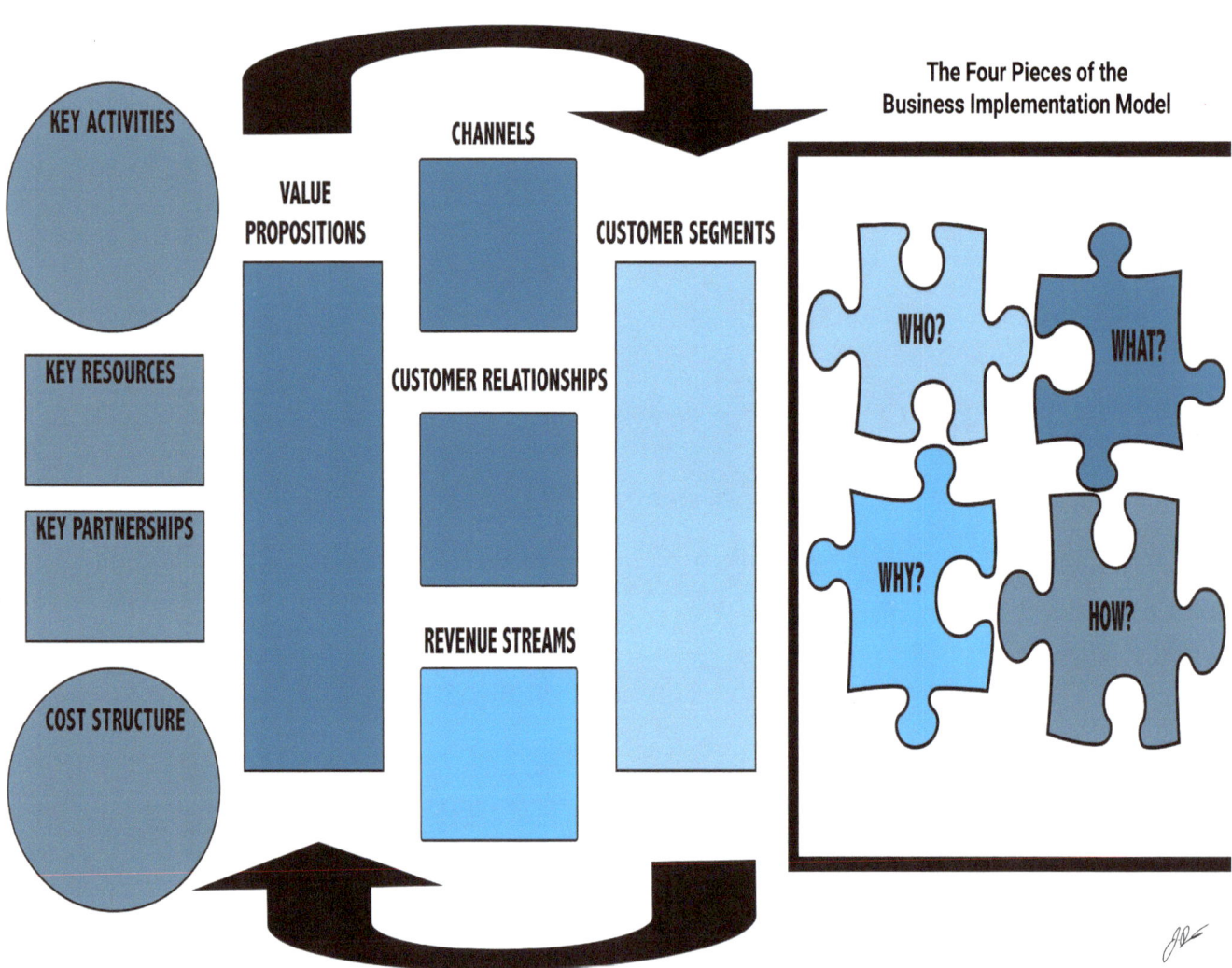

The Complete Business Model Design Canvas

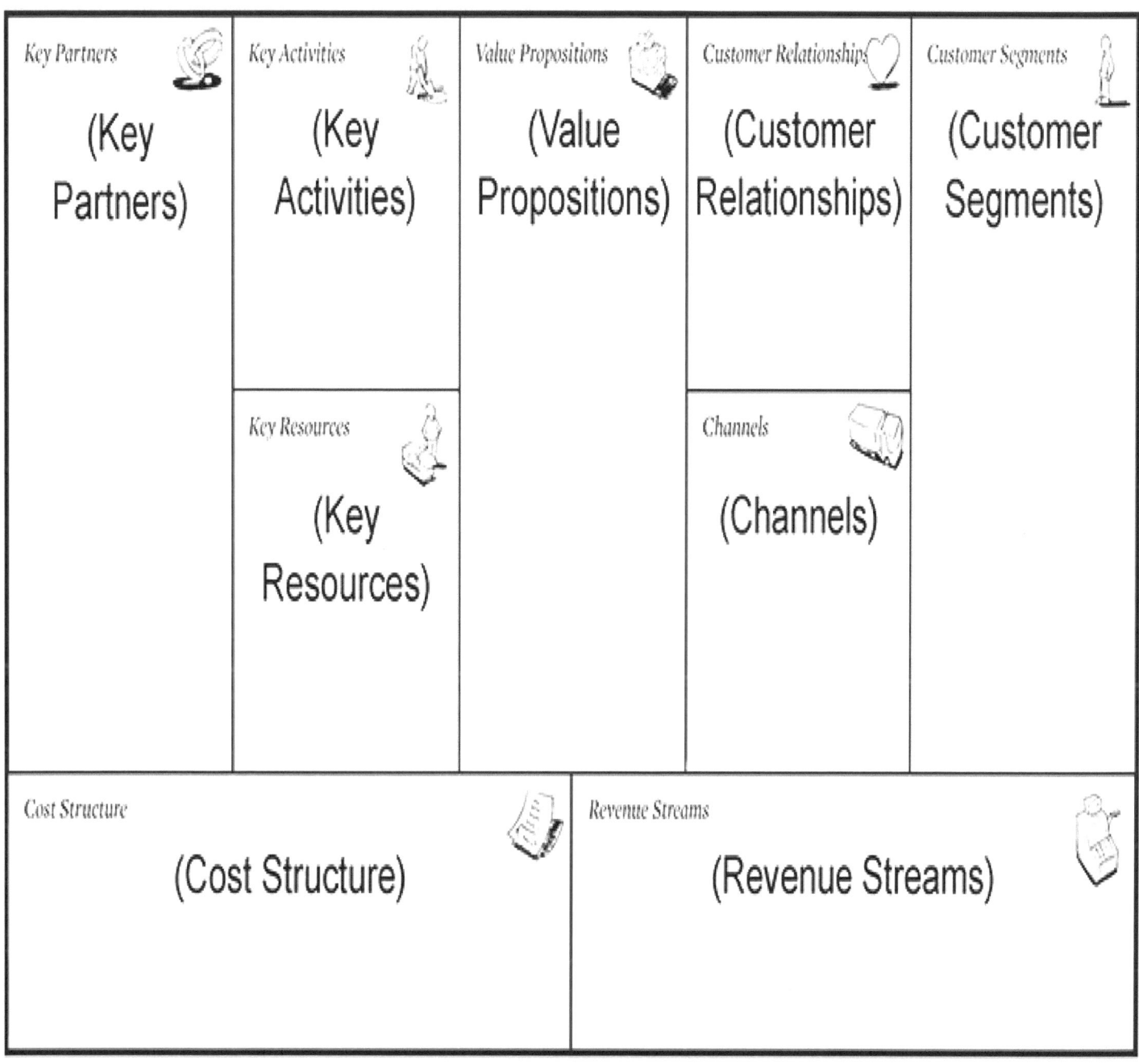

Standard Business Model Canvas

SWOT Analysis

Assessing: _____

	Helpful	Harmful
Internal	**Strengths** What do you do better than others? What Unique capabilities and resources do you posses? What do others believe are your strengths? What is your Competitive Advantage? Value Propositions?	**Weaknesses** What do your competitors do better? What can you improve given your current model? What do others note as your weaknesses? Disadvantages to others?
External	**Opportunity** What trends or conditions may have a positive impact? What elements can your business exploit to its advantage?	**Threats** What trends or conditions may have a negative impact? What are your competitors doing that may impact business? Do you have solid financial support? Do your weaknesses add to your threats? Environmental troubles?

Value Ladder

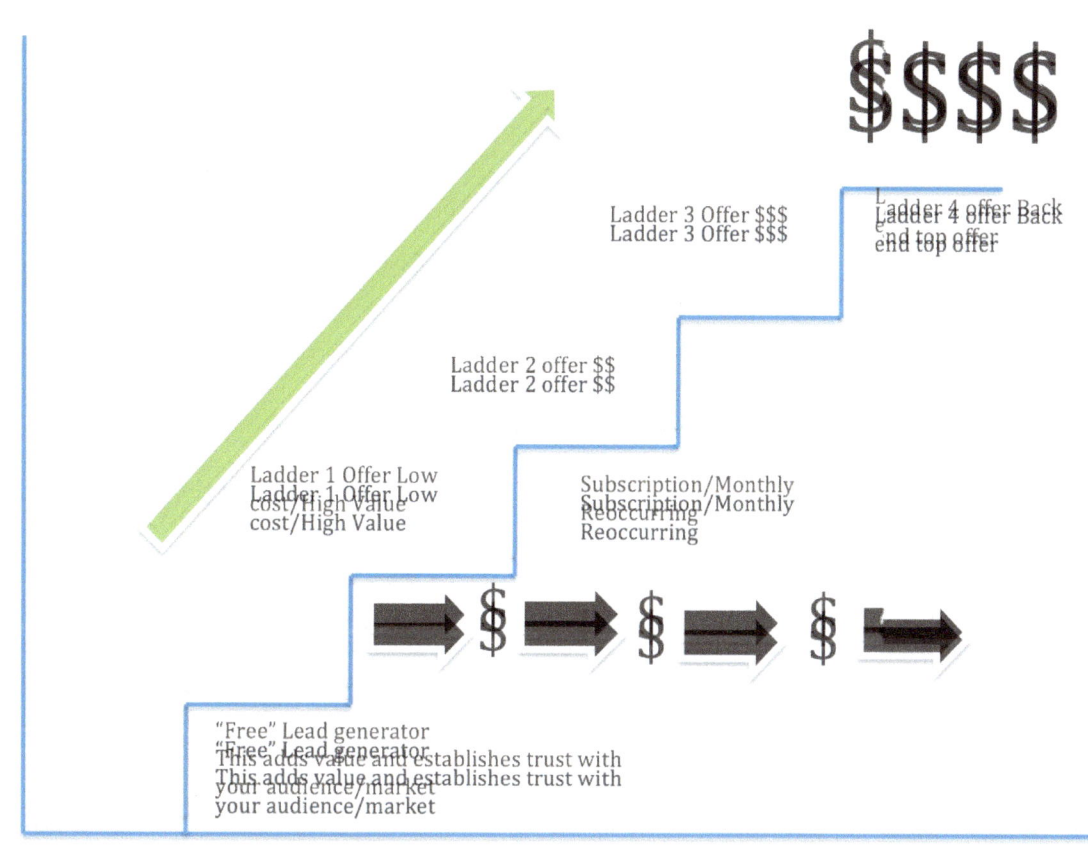

Your value ladder is the essence of your sales funnel, whether you're an eCommerce business, brick and motor, or a combination of both. Understanding your value ladder is essential when establishing and deploying your sales funnel.

For example, I worked with an air conditioning client for several years with their value ladder/sales funnel.

If you're familiar with the industry, great. You may know that for a very long time, many companies struggled with how to generate interested leads without going door to door or making cold calls.

Working with this company, I helped them establish partnerships with local grocery stores where we were able to place a table inside the stores and utilize the foot traffic inside the stores to generate leads.

This proved to work exceptionally well and became a primary source of lead generation, the initial steps to your value ladder/sales funnel.

Every value ladder/sales funnel will have different offers depending on the business value offerings. The two things that will always be similar is the initial lead generating component of **"free"** no risk and the top tier, most expensive value offer.

Sales Funnel

The Cash Flow Quadrant is a concept created by Robert Kiyosaki that breaks down the flow of cash to a person based on their role within a system (Business). It's written at an elementary level so even a 5th grader can comprehend. It's a very important concept to know and apply to your life and your business. It will help you understand your employees' motivations as well as your own motivations.

CASHFLOW QUADRANT

4 WAYS TO PRODUCE INCOME
LINEAR INCOME VS. LEVERAGED & RESIDUAL INCOME

E

Employee
YOU HAVE A J.O.B.
NO LEVERAGE : 5% WEALTH
The amount of active work determines income.

 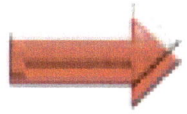 

TIME = $$$

B

Business Owner
YOU OWN A SYSTEM
LEVERAGE : 95% WEALTH
Income does not depend on active work.

 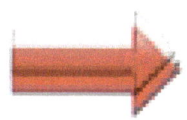 

PEOPLE WORK WITH YOU = $$$$$$$$$

S

Self-Employed
YOU OWN A J.O.B.
NO LEVERAGE : 95% POPULATION
The amount of active work determines income.

 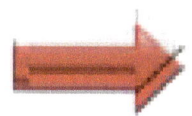 

TIME = $$$

I

Investor
YOU OWN INVESTMENTS
LEVERAGE : 5% POPULATION
Income does not depend on active work.

 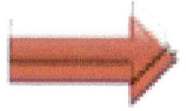 

YOUR MONEY WORKS FOR YOU = $$$$$$$$$

This Toolkit is to help you Strategize your business model, understand your Customer's Needs, or Pain Points, and develop an action plan to Implement.

Taking the time to conduct these Strategize and plan out your business will give you a great advantage on your competition and a sound understanding to your value propositions as well as your customer needs. Connecting with your customers and their needs will open your business up to the growth potential it has.